Climbing High

Written by Andy Seed

Contents

1	What is rock climbing?	2
2	Types of rock climbing	4
3	Equipment	8
4	Skills	12
5	The history of rock climbing	16
6	Famous climbers – past and present	20
7	Ready to rock?	24
8	Extreme rock climbing	26
	Glossary	28
	Index	29
	The steps of rock climbing	30

Collins

1 What is rock climbing?

Rock climbing is all about getting to the top!

Climbers try to reach the summit without falling –
either on rock faces outdoors or on indoor
climbing walls. Rock climbing needs strength,
fitness, balance and good mental focus.
It's all worth it for the amazing feeling
climbers get when they reach the top.

Rock climbing is becoming more
and more popular as a sport and is even
an event in the Olympic Games.
It's not just for adults – many
children enjoy climbing too.

The best climbers in the world
take on huge cliffs, steep
mountains and
difficult overhangs.
They are often rewarded
with a stunning view
when they reach
the summit.

3

2 Types of rock climbing

There are several kinds of rock climbing to choose from.

Indoor walls

Many people begin climbing on indoor walls. It's a safe place to learn the sport as it has all the equipment, plus trained instructors watching over the climbers.

There are many types of climbing walls and some are very challenging. Each wall has a collection of climbing **holds** which are colour-coded for the different levels of difficulty.

Bouldering

Some people like to climb up small rock faces or boulders. This is called bouldering. Climbers don't have any safety equipment apart from padded mats in case they fall.

Many indoor climbing centres have walls especially for bouldering, which are up to six metres high. Climbers often put chalk on their fingers to improve their grip.

Some bouldering challenges include an overhang.

Outdoor climbing

Outdoor climbers climb rock faces on cliffs, hills
and mountains. They're usually attached to a rope
fixed to the rock to keep them safe if they fall.

The rope here is fixed to the rock above the climber.

Mountain climbing

This often involves walking, scrambling and climbing
with ropes. It might even include ice climbing, where
climbers use special axes and **crampons** to grip snow and ice.

Competitions and sport climbing

Sport climbers compete in high-intensity climbing on fairly short routes. Some competitions are about climbing a wall in the fastest time, and others follow special tricky routes.

The fastest climbers can reach the top of a 15-metre wall in under seven seconds!

3 Equipment

Rock climbers use all kinds of gear. Some equipment is to help them climb better and some is for safety.

Helmet

Protects climbers from falling rocks outdoors and keeps their head safe if they slip or fall.

Chalk bag

Holds chalk dust which helps climbers to grip rock.

Carabiners

Metal loops used to connect ropes and other equipment.

Quickdraws

These connect ropes to bolts fixed into rock faces.

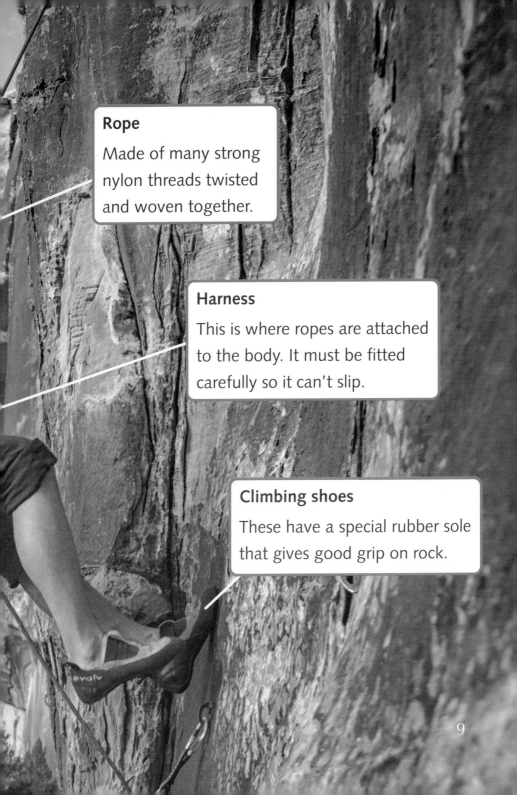

Rope

Made of many strong nylon threads twisted and woven together.

Harness

This is where ropes are attached to the body. It must be fitted carefully so it can't slip.

Climbing shoes

These have a special rubber sole that gives good grip on rock.

9

Belaying

Rock climbers are usually attached to a rope as they climb. The rope passes through a **device** fixed to the rock and the other end is held by a fellow climber on the ground, called the belayer.

The rope is attached to their harness in a belay device so they can catch a fall. The belayer can also lower the climber to the ground.

A belay device acts like a brake on the rope.

belay device

Knots

Climbers must know which knots to use where. The figure of eight knot is very important as it helps to keep climbers safe when they are being belayed. It is one of the knots used to tie in a rope to a harness.

See if you can tie a figure of eight knot by following the guide below!

How to tie a figure of eight knot

1

2

3

4

4 Skills

Puzzle solving

Part of the fun of rock climbing is that it's like solving a puzzle. Climbers must look for the best route and work out where to place their hands and feet.

Climbers love edges and cracks on a rock face! They can be used to grip – and anchors can be fixed in cracks for attaching ropes.

Basic techniques

If you want to climb, you must learn to:

- push with your legs, not pull with your arms
- use the correct part of the foot on each foothold
- grip with straight arms, where possible
- stay close to the wall.

Even a very small edge can be used for grip.

Climbing challenge

How would you climb this wall? Where would you place your hands and feet to reach the top?

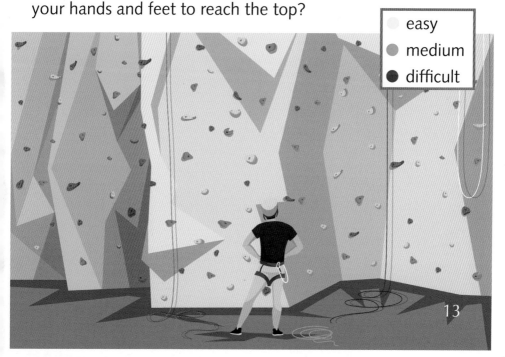

○ easy
● medium
● difficult

Grades

Climbing routes are often graded to help climbers know how difficult they are. Most countries have their own system of grades, like this one, used in the UK:

Easy
Moderate
Difficult
Very difficult
Severe
Very severe
Extremely severe

This climb is certainly not "Easy"!

Abseiling

Abseiling is the quickest way you can get down from the top of a climb or descend a cliff to begin climbing back up.

If you are climbing with a partner who's belaying you, they control the belay device so that you can abseil down.

If you are on your own, you control the device to lower yourself, using a rope fixed to the top of the rock face. The belay device uses **friction** to stop the rope from slipping and allows you to adjust the speed you're dropping.

Safety

As well as being fun, rock climbing can also be dangerous. It's important to:

- use the correct equipment

- go with an experienced partner

- choose a climbing route that suits your ability

- check all ropes, knots, anchors, harnesses and other pieces of equipment to make sure they are fitted properly

- always pay attention to what is going on

- take rests.

Did you know?

Rock climbing makes your hands grow! The muscles that give you grip grow as they are used a lot.

5 The history of rock climbing

How it began

People have climbed mountains for centuries, but as a sport, rock climbing is quite young. Mountaineering became popular in the 1800s and it was then that some climbers in Europe began to tackle steep or vertical rock faces.

Some of these climbers used chisels to make holds in the rock or hammered metal spikes called **pitons** into cracks. Even ladders were used sometimes!

Some early climbers wore ordinary shoes.

Women climbers

As mountaineering and climbing became more popular, many women wanted to try it. They were often not encouraged by men, so women started their own climbing groups. The Ladies Scottish Climbing Club was founded in 1908. Its members wore long, heavy tweed skirts, jackets and hats to climb! These not only made climbing difficult but would not be thought of as safe today.

Rock climbing timeline

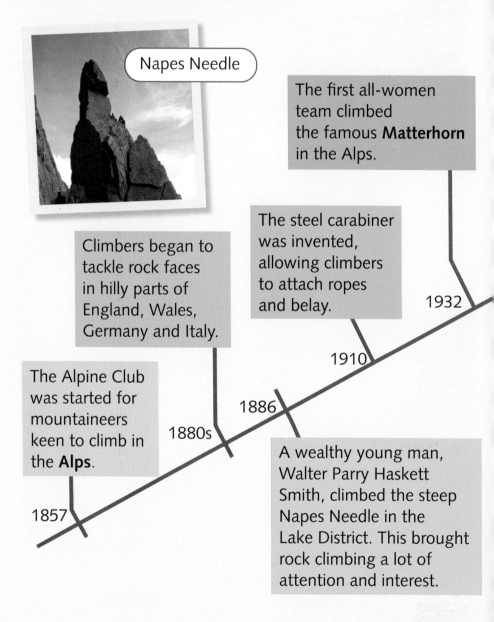

Napes Needle

The first all-women team climbed the famous **Matterhorn** in the Alps.

The steel carabiner was invented, allowing climbers to attach ropes and belay.

Climbers began to tackle rock faces in hilly parts of England, Wales, Germany and Italy.

The Alpine Club was started for mountaineers keen to climb in the **Alps**.

A wealthy young man, Walter Parry Haskett Smith, climbed the steep Napes Needle in the Lake District. This brought rock climbing a lot of attention and interest.

1857

1880s

1886

1910

1932

The 900-metre **El Capitan** cliff in the USA was climbed using metal bolts. It took a team 45 days in total.

The first sport climbing World Championships was held.

1991

1973

1964

Stretchy Lycra clothing started to become popular, making climbing easier.

1958

1940

The first indoor climbing wall was built in Leeds, England. It helped climbers to train in winter when outdoor conditions were difficult.

Stronger and safer ropes made of nylon became available.

El Capitan

Matterhorn

6 Famous climbers – past and present

Lucy Walker (1836–1916)

This British mountaineer became the first woman to climb the 4478-metre Matterhorn in 1871. This made her famous at a time when many people believed that only men could climb high mountains.

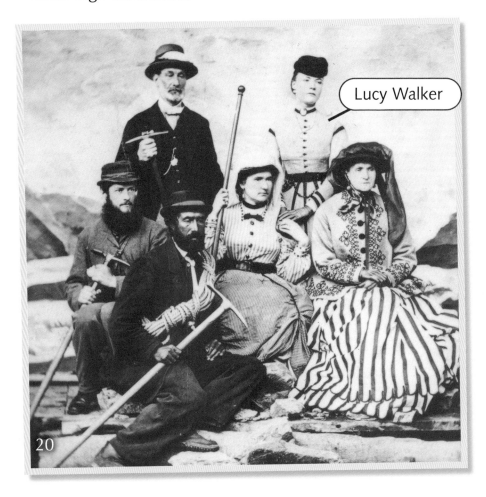

Lucy Walker

Walter Bonatti (1930–2011)

Unlike many early climbers, Walter Bonatti came from a poor background. He could not afford expensive equipment, but the Italian climber didn't let this hold him back. In 1954, he was part of the first team to reach the summit of K2 in the **Himalayas**, the second-highest mountain in the world.

Mark Wellman
(born 1960)

The American wheelchair user has climbed some of the toughest rock faces in the world, using only his arms. Mark and his climbing partner Mike Corbett have also developed several devices to help disabled people enjoy rock climbing. One of these, called the Adaptive Pull-up Bar, allows climbers to pull themselves up a rope.

Alex Honnold
(born 1985)

This skilled American made an astonishing climb in 2017 when he scaled the 880-metre face of the famous El Capitan rock in California, without using ropes or other equipment. It took him nearly four hours to reach the top.

Ashima Shiraishi (born 2001)

Ashima began climbing at the age of just six in the USA.
Experts believe that she's the best teenage climber
in the world. She's won the Bouldering World Youth
Championships three times.

7 Ready to rock?

It's great to start rock climbing young. Many of the best rock climbers began indoors when they were between four and seven years old. Some **rock gyms** have special starter bouldering walls which young children can use.

Climbing not only makes you stronger, but it's all about tackling challenges. This helps you become better at thinking problems through – not just when climbing, but in everyday life!

Did you know?

The highest mountain in Africa, Mount Kilimanjaro, was climbed by a six-year-old girl in 2019!

On a **traverse** wall you climb along rather than up.

Join a club

You can meet other climbers at climbing clubs and learn together. The instructors will help you gain different skills and overcome problems, so you can climb higher and harder walls.

Climbing clubs are a good place to make new friends, build confidence and have fun!

Instructors will show you rope skills and how to stay safe.

Dealing with fear

Many people have a fear of heights and it's normal to find high places scary. Rock climbing is a great way to overcome these fears. It helps you learn to be bold and to stay calm in difficult situations.

8 Extreme rock climbing

Maybe you'd like to aim for some extreme challenges like these one day ...

Don't try this at home!

Big wall climbing

Do you fancy climbing a long, high rock face? You might have to sleep in a tent attached to the cliff, called a hanging **bivouac**!

Great Sail Peak, Baffin Island, Canada

Free soloing

This is for the most fearless of climbers – no ropes or safety equipment are used! It needs great strength, skill and bravery.

Table Mountain South Africa

Deep water soloing

This is like free soloing, but on sea cliffs. You know that if you fall you'll land in water, so it's a bit less dangerous!

Majorca

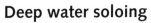

Japan

Speed climbing

Do you dare race to the top? The fast and furious sport of speed climbing is now part of the Olympic Games.

Glossary

Alps a group of high mountains in Europe

bivouac a camp where people sleep outdoors

crampons spiked metal grips on shoes used to help people climb over ice and snow

device an invention or piece of equipment that does a job

El Capitan a huge rock face in North America

friction friction happens when two objects rub together, slowing something down

Himalayas the highest mountains in the world, in Asia

holds places that people put their hands and feet when climbing

Matterhorn a very high, steep mountain in the Alps

pitons metal spikes hammered into rocks to help climbers climb

rock gyms buildings with lots of indoor climbing walls

severe extreme or very bad or difficult

traverse to move across

Index

Alps 18

anchors 12, 15

belaying 10–11, 14, 18

big wall climbing 26

Bonatti, Walter 21

bouldering 5, 23, 24

carabiners 8, 18

climbing walls 2, 4, 19

deep water soloing 27

El Capitan 19, 22

equipment 4–5, 8–9, 15, 21, 22, 26

free soloing 26–27

harnesses 9–11, 15

Himalayas 21

Honnold, Alex 22

ice climbing 6

knots 11, 15

Lake District 18

Matterhorn 18–20

Mount Kilimanjaro 24

Napes Needle 18

Olympic Games 2, 27

overhangs 2, 5

ropes 6, 8–12, 15, 18–19, 22, 25–26

safety 5, 8, 15, 26

Shiraishi, Ashima 23

speed climbing 27

sport climbing 7, 19

traverse wall 24

Walker, Lucy 20

Wellman, Mark 22

The steps of rock climbing

1. Choose your location.

2. Collect your equipment.

3. Meet your belayer.

4. Do your safety checks.

5. Practise your skills!

❧ Ideas for reading ❧

Written by Gill Matthews
Primary Literacy Consultant

Reading objectives:

- read books that are structured in different ways and read for a range of purposes
- check that the text makes sense, discussing understanding and explaining the meaning of words in context
- retrieve and record information from non-fiction

Spoken language objectives:

- give well-structured descriptions, explanations and narratives for different purposes, including for expressing feelings
- maintain attention and participate actively in collaborative conversations, staying on topic and initiating and responding to comments
- participate in discussions, presentations, performances, role play, improvisations and debates

Curriculum links: Science – Rocks; Geography – Place knowledge

Interest words: bivouac, crampons, device, holds, pitons

Resources: atlas or map of the world

Build a context for reading

- Look at the front cover. Ask children what kind of book they think this is and what it might be about.
- Read the back cover blurb. Ask children what they know about rock climbing and what they can work out from looking at the cover.
- Ask children where they can find out more about what is in the book. Turn to the contents page and ask where they think they can find out more about what rock climbing is.

Understand and apply reading strategies

- Read pp2–3 aloud. Use questioning to explore children's understanding of this chapter and what rock climbing involves.
- Ask questions about pp2–3 that involve children finding and retrieving information.